RAILROAD PHOTOGRAPHY

Western States

ROBERT O. HALE

Compiled by Donald Duke

Golden West Books

RAILROAD PHOTOGRAPHY

Western States
Robert O. Hale

Copyright © 2004 by Donald Duke
All Rights Reserved

Published by Golden West Books
San Marino, California 91118 U.S.A.

Library of Congress Catalog Card No. 2004060683
I.S.B.N. No. 0-87095-120-3

Library of Congress Cataloging-in-Publication Data

Hale, Robert O., 1912-1992
    Railroad Photography : Western States / Robert O. Hale.
      p. cm.
    ISBN 0-87095-120-3
      1. Photography of railroads—West (U.S.)   2. Railroads—West (U.S.)—Pictorial works.
    I. Title.

TR715.H35 2004
385'.0978'022—dc22   2004060683

TITLE PAGE ILLUSTRATION

Undoubtedlly the handsomest diesel locomotive to hit the Santa Fe rails were Alco's PA passenger units. In this scene, Nos. 66 and 57 twist the *Grand Canyon Limited* around Sullivan's curve just west of Cajon Station on the eastbound line. It was quiet here before this photograph was taken, until the throbbing of diesel units announced the arrival of Alco PA's at 3:55 P.M. — N35720

COVER ILLUSTRATION

The sound of a freight, headed by a cab-forward, breaks the air as it lifts this trains from the Martinez Station and it is climbing the grade to Suisun Point. Here the freight will cross the long double-track Martinez-Benicia railway bridge. — N36748

Golden West Books

P.O. Box 80250
San Marino, California • 91118-8250

The *Super Chief*, Santa Fe's all-Pullman premier train is due to arrive at Los Angeles Union Passenger Terminal at 9:00 A.M. sharp. Bob Hale photographed the *Super Chief* during June at 6:30 A.M. as it was rolling down the west side of Cajon Pass just north of Cajon Station. — N35908

Table of Contents

"Trains Magazine dips into the files of a talented photographer for a fresh look at railroading as observed through the extraordinary camera of Robert Hale."

David P. Morgan - Editor
Trains Magazine
October 1956

ROBERT O. HALE
1912-1992

The railroad and the steam locomotive has excited generations, ever since the steel wheel rolled on the steel rail. It is not difficult to understand why this has been so. The sheer impact of the sight and sound of the mighty locomotive was a sight to behold.

In the more than two decades since the conclusion of World War II, American railroads went through what has been an exciting transformation, the change from the steam locomotive to diesel-electric motive power. By the end of the 1950's, steam power had essentially vanished from the America railroad scene.

To record this great metamorphosis in the American West was a young Navy photographer stationed at the San Diego Naval Base by the name of Robert O. Hale. As a Navy photographer he not only had an eye for a picture, but access to the best of photographic equipment. At this same time, there was a renaissance in photographic equipment, with faster lenses, and faster film. This led Hale into experimentation of nighttime railroad photography and the panning of railroad shots where the subject would be frozen and the background blurred.

Bob Hale found everything in the West was big. Big mountains, big deserts, big distances, big grades and canyons, and above all big steam and mighty diesel-electric locomotives. To haul these big tonnages of freight and passengers, were big railroads such as the Santa Fe, Southern Pacific, and Union Pacific.

When it comes to railroad photography, there are railroad photographers, and then there are railroad picture makers. Robert O. Hale certainly was a picture maker. This book then, is a photography album of his Western railroad scenes of locomotives and trains, of railroad people and railroad places.

Robert O. Hale was born in Gentryville, Indiana, on January 21, 1912. At an early age his family left Indiana and moved to Kentucky. His mother, Nelda, soon divorced his father, Cully Hale, and in due course married a railroad man. His stepfather worked in the roundhouse of some railroad in Louisville, Kentucky. His new father took young Bob to the roundhouse to see the real locomotives. He enjoyed his trips to the rail yards and before long the railroad bug had bitten Bob Hale.

With money saved from selling magazines, door to door, Bob purchased his first camera and began taking pictures of trains. He also had an interest in music. At age eleven he took up the bugle and got pretty good at it. At age twelve he joined the Boy Scouts and became the troop official bugler. Hale continued to practice the bugle and entered several bugle contests. While in high school he became the best teenage bugler of Kentucky. All the while he continued his railroad photography.

Upon graduating from high school in 1928, most graduates found it impossible to find a job with little experience and no funds for college. The Depression was in the making, so Bob joined the Navy, at least he would eat well. He went to boot camp at Great Lake Naval Training Center, and before long became the base bugler. He was convinced to join the base band. He was impressed with the drum major who led the band, and took training for drum major. With assignments being passed out, he was ready to see the world. Being in the band he could not be assigned to a ship. Several band members were assigned to the Canal Zone duty in Panama. His duty was fire control. With few fires, the job became boring. During his free time several band members formed a small group and played at a night club on the base. One of the band members was a banjo player. Looking like fun, so Bob became a self-taught banjo player.

Bob was reassigned to the San Diego Naval Base as a Chief Petty Officer - fire control. Shortly thereafter, he advanced to Chief Petty Officer - Quartermaster. All the time Bob continued taking railroad pictures and continued his interest in music. Hale dreamed of becoming a commercial photographer upon retirement from the Navy. To break into music he knew would be difficult.

On his retirement from the Navy, Bob following his dream of becoming a commercial photographer, he attended a four year course at Art Center School of Photography, a prestigious photo school in Los Angeles. In the middle of his course, the Korean War started and Bob was called back to active duty with rank of Chief Petty Officer - Photographer. He was in his prime, taking all types of photographs and access to all kinds of photographic equipment.

Bob was taking all kinds of photographs of the Santa Fe around the San Diego region and up the Pacific Coast. Hale soon moved to Cajon Pass and the Tehachapi region for variety. While still single, he made Cajon Pass his weekend home. Hale struck up a friendship with Summit train order operator Chard Walker. Chard was also single and made his home in the Los Angeles Railway funeral car, the *Descanso*, the clubhouse of the Los Angeles based Railroad Boosters.

The *Descanso* was presented to the Railroad Boosters just prior to World War II by the Los Angeles Railway. The Boosters decided to take it to the Summit of Cajon as a club house and train watching platform. The *Descanso* was used mainly on weekends for members. The interior had been gutted out and was

Bob Hale climbs into the cab of Union Pacific turbine No. 57 while at Summit, just to see what the inside of the cab looked like. - N37242

equipped with army bunk beds, a desk, table, stove, icebox, and a coal stove for heat. All the comforts of home!

As a member of Railroad Boosters I often visited the *Descanso*. During the war there was no fuel to drive to Summit, so some of us took the train. Bob Drenk, who was station agent for the Santa Fe at Fullerton planned our trips. We would take the Santa Fe *California Limited* from Los Angeles to Summit. Sum-

In this nighttime time exposure by Bob Hale, he shows what the Railroad Booster clubhouse the *Descanso* looked like on the side of Summit Mountain. In this view, Dick Steinheimer sits on the steps of the car. Note the large door where the casket was shoved in.

The *Descanso* was Chard Walker's home for several years while a dispatcher at Summit. This interior view shows how complete the car was. All the comforts of home. - N37595

mit was a scheduled flag stop. Most trains, especially the streamliners speed by Summit, taking their orders on the fly. Bob Hale was often there, with a car, and full of conversation.

On our return home it was a different operation. Although a flag stop, and orders had been given to stop to pick up passengers at Summit, trains would speed through. We would stand out and give the washout sign, and would often have to throw rocks at the engineer to get his attention. Sometimes the train would stop way down the track and we would have to run to catch it.

Bob began experimenting with nighttime railroad photography in San Diego. He would set up his camera at open flash, then walk around a still train flashing his flash gun at the locomotive, wheels, cab, and some of the cars. This experimental photography produced great results. I believe he used flash bulbs at times. Bob continued his nighttime shots at Summit using multiflash from stands.

One memorable time exposure was made at the Tehachapi Loop. Bob set up his camera just above the Loop and opened the camera lens for a time exposure. The camera was pointed down the canyon toward Woodford. With a pitch black night, a train was spotted at Woodford, so he opened the lens. The train took 15 minutes to reach the Loop. Then Hale closed the shutter. The results was a picture like taken at dusk, with the trains path in lights.

A Graflex Company official saw Bob Hales' shot at Tehachapi and was impressed. The photo won Bob a Graflex award and the picture was used in their

This nighttime time exposure won Bob Hale a Graflex Photographic Award. It is a time exposure made at Tehachapi Loop. - N35679

advertising.

I began to experiment with nighttime railroad photography using a flash gun with wires strung out and flash bulbs enclosed in pie tins for reflections. I happened to visit Andrews Hardware in downtown Los Angeles and ran into a photo bluff, I told him what I was trying to accomplish. He said, "did you ever use magnesium wire?" He showed me what it would do. You light it, and it went poof, producing light, a huge amount of light. Magnesium wire was used to set off dynamite at a distance.

I tried it in Pacific Electric's subway and terminal. We strung it out down the tube. It went off producing more than enough light in the subway. I am sure the motorman thought the world was coming to an end. I showed it to Bob Hale who used it on several Cajon Pass shots. The supply of magnesium wire ran out and we were unable to get anymore.

The Base Commander of the San Diego Naval Base ask Bob to make an educational film based on the treatment and care of a handicapped child. Apparently one of the Commander's children was handicapped. It was during that time that Bob ran into his future wife, Margaret. She was a trained professional physical therapist working with the child. Bob and Margaret worked together on the film. They began to date, fell in love, and were married August 18, 1955. That more or less ended Bob's weekend trips to Cajon and Tehachapi.

Following the Korean conflict, Hale again retired from the Navy. Apparently, he never did finish his course at the Art Center School of Photography. Searching for a job, he found one at the Southern Pacific Pipeline Company. The Southern Pacific was laying a fuel pipeline along the Sunset Route between Los Angeles and El Paso, Texas. Hale's job was to photograph the construction

of the pipeline. The pipeline also followed the Southern Pacific tracks thus providing Hale a chance to photograph the last steam on the Sunset Route.

Following his assignment with the Southern Pacific, Hale got a job with the Army Corps of Engineers as a photographer of flood control projects in Northern California between 1955 and 1972. During his free time in Northern California he photographed the Northwestern Pacific, the California Western, and the Southern Pacific in the Cascades.

In the 1960's Hale supplied *Trains Magazine* with articles using his photographs, many using his nighttime techniques. Most memorable was an article of photographs taken at Los Angeles Union Passenger Terminal at night. It showed the station in many scenes, and the train operation. It was outstanding.

David Morgan, longtime editor of *Trains Magazine*, classified Bob's work as unique and innovative. This was mainly due to his nighttime photographs

Bob Hale was known for his nighttime time exposures. Here is the *Southern Pacific Coaster*, train No. 69, at Los Angeles Union Station. - N36895

and panned train scenes. Hale's photography work also appeared in my railroad books.

I published a book called *Night Train* in 1961. This was a book of all nighttime railroad photos, I called on Bob to help me out with some of his outstanding photographs, which he did, including steam, diesel and electric shots.

About this time he met Richard Steinheimer, another master railroad photographer. Steinheimer was a photographer for the Glendale *News-Press*. He had sent me a picture he made for the paper of a Southern Pacific piggyback train by panning. The process is to set the camera at slow speed and then follow the train along and snap the shutter. The train would be frozen and the background blurred. Bob Hale was impressed and learned how to duplicate the process.

Panned photographs were Bob Hale's specialty. In this scene, Southern Pacific No. 4421 roars northbound up the San Joaquin Valley with the *San Joaquin Daylight*. - N36859

Bob and Margaret needed a vacation. They decided to drive to Canada, swing through the east and return by the Denver & Rio Grande main line and narrow-gauge. Their purpose was to capture the last of steam in Canada, the east, and the west. Hale also took pictures of diesels, but his love was the steam locomotive.

On his large trip around the United States, Bob experimented with the panned shot. Bob would entice Margaret to drive the car while he would set himself in the back seat, head out the window pacing a train. The locomotive and cars would be frozen, the wheel action fuzzy , and the background blurred. After the long tour he submitted several articles to *Trains Magazine*.

What type of camera did Bob Hale use? When I knew him he was using a Speed Graphic 4x5. He also used 4x5 Graflex, the camera with a large hood you look down into. Photograph A-74 shows Bob alongside a Graphic View Camera 4x5. In the late 1960's everything was going to 2 1/4 square roll film camera like a Rolliflex. He even used the 35mm camera.

The end of the steam locomotive in the United States more or less ended his railroad photography. He did shoot first and second generation diesels because they were there. He like Santa Fe's *Chief* and *Super Chief*, as well as Union Pacific's *City of Los Angeles*. Bob Hale thought the American Locomotive PA (passenger) and FA (freight) diesel locomotives to be classics.

Bob and Margaret Hale finally retired to Sun City, Arizona, where they planned to live out their Golden Years. He kept physically fit with physical exercise and took to bicycle riding. After a bout with pneumonia in 1986, it was

While photographing the Union Pacific main line, Bob Hale checks his camera while standing in the vestibule of "Big Boy" No. 4010. - N37401

disclosed that Hale had Vasculitis and Myelodysplasia a bone marrow cancer. Bob fought the disease, but lost the battle on July 11, 1992.

There are many prints taken by Bob Hale out there. His camera work has been preserved by Malcolm McCarter, P. O. Box 1569, Camp Verde, Arizona 86322-1569. McCarter makes 8x10 prints from Hale's negatives for a nominal price. He offers Hale's work in addition to thousands of railroad photography by the masters. If a particular photograph appearing in this book interests you, look for the negative number at the end of each caption.

Donald Duke
Publisher
Golden West Books

Southern Pacific's *West Coast Limited*, operating between Los Angeles and Portland, Oregon, is shown from the roof of the Terminal Annex. Note the No. 4451 has a hot boiler as the safety valve is blowing off steam. Also, note the streaks of light from baggage tractors moving about. Train No. 69 was due out of Los Angeles Union Terminal at 7:30 P.M. each evening. Santa Fe's *San Diegan* is loading passengers on the right. - N36895

LOS ANGELES UNION PASSENGER TERMINAL

Here is where the West begins - at the Los Angeles Union Passenger Terminal, a place where passenger train drumhead signs glow in the dark. It is called a terminal because tracks are not continuous, they dead end. The Los Angeles Union Passenger Terminal is the last of the great railroad stations to be built in the United States. It officially opened on Sunday, May 7, 1939, followed by a magnificent parade of motive power along Alameda Street, and a pageant at the terminal tracks. The station opened just in time to become the arrival and departure point for hundreds of servicemen bound for the Pacific theatre during World War II.

Architecturally beautiful and typically California mission in style, the station is both spacious and ultramodern in every way. Built at a cost of eleven million dollars by the three railroads which served Southern California - Santa Fe, Southern Pacific, and the Union Pacific.

From the outside, the station buildings' appearance suggest early California, with a giant clock tower of Moorish orientation. In front of the station itself, you have high windows lighting ticket sales, together with a slanting red tile roof. The arcades on each side of the station are complete with patios, with trees

Los Angeles Union Passenger Terminal is seen from the gallery of the Los Angeles City Hall tower. This nighttime scene shows the complete station, the terminal tracks behind the station, and the United States Post Office Terminal Annex on the left. I have no idea how long a time this time exposure was to light up this entire scene. - N36328

of orange, palm and pepper - routed in native soils, surrounded with flowers.

The station building, tracks and ramps to the tracks, cover an area of 48 acres. The station itself extends 850 feet along Alameda Street. The great entrance to the station opens upon an impressive hall with a magnificent arched ceiling, with mosaic floors created from marble from around the world.

Robert Hale found the Los Angeles Union Passenger Terminal fascinating and worthy of nighttime and daytime photographs. He decided this station had to be photographed by this nighttime technique. With a steady camera mounted on a tripod, and open shutter he went to work photographing every nook and cranny of the station. From trackside, his camera captured unusual scenes.

Shadows lost to the intensity of blackness were lighted as Bob moved

This scene shows two Santa Fe trains in the terminal. The *Super Chief* is in the immediate foreground, the *San Diegan* at the right. - N36017

around the platforms as his camera captured steam escaping from safety valves on locomotives, men racing around on tractors loading mail into baggage car, and platforms loaded with Railway Express.

Out at the station throat, the departure and arrival of passenger trains are marked with streaks of light. Hale went so far as to climb to the gallery of Los Angeles City Hall to take an overall time exposure of the complete station.

Hale captured the north end of the station from the roof of the United States Post Office Terminal Annex building. He took many record shots in and around the station during daylight hours with the coming and goings of passenger trains.

With the creation of Amtrak in 1971, the three railroads serving the station went out of the passenger business. Train arrivals and departures were slim, until the coming of the Metropolitan Transit Authority Red Line subway and Pasadena Gold Line. Metrolink, the commuter railroad provides the station with more arrivals and departures than during the height of World War II, in addition to Amtraks' San Diego to Santa Barbara trains.

With a switcher locomotive waiting for the departure of an unknown streamliner from Track One, the headlight shows the path from the terminal out near Mission Tower, as the train passes the camera with open shutter. - N36335 (RIGHT) The backside of LAUPT as seen from the roof of the Terminal Annex. This scene shows the lighted ticket office with the big windows, and the Pullman Company offices to the right or in the foreground. Also visible is the lighted clock tower, and Los Angeles City Hall in the distance. - N36330

Santa Fe's *San Diegan* was photographed passing Terminal Tower while en route to San Diego. Note the car next to the tail end with the owl eye windows. This was an experimental, one of a kind car, called the Pendulum car. - N35989

Motive-power for Santa Fe's *Chief* backs up from Mission Tower into the inner terminal. The fireman looks to the rear calling signals to the engineer. - N35827

Union Pacific's *City of Los Angeles* leaves Los Angeles Union Passenger Terminal behind four experimental test locomotives called ALCO PA's. - N35684

One of the most revolutionary trends of modern railroading was the introduction of the streamliner. From the very beginning the *San Diegan* was an institution. In the scene, San Diego bound *San Diegan* has just left Del Mar behind diesel locomotive No. 4. The Del Mar pier is in the distance. - N35697

SANTA FE'S
Los Angeles to San Diego Surf Line

After climbing the Linda Vista grade north of San Diego, it was all down hill to Del Mar. After reaching the coast, the *San Diegan* races toward Del Mar station behind triple PA ALCO diesels. - N35990

Santa Fe's Surf Line was constructed during 1888 between Los Angeles to San Diego, as a quick way between the two destinations. Previously a line was run between San Diego and San Bernardino by way of Temecula Canyon. Which had previously washed out several times. The Surf Line between Los Angeles, Santa Ana, San Clemente, Del Mar and San Diego was completed for service on August 12, 1888. Passenger and freight service was minimal as San Diego did not contain many inhabitants.

San Diego had a spectacular victorian-styled station on Broadway which was larger than its' population. This depot was torn down for the Panama-California Exposition, celebrating the completion of the Panama Canal, and was replaced with a huge Spanish Renaissance-style depot which stands today.

Passenger and freight service was minimal until war clouds gathered prior to World War II. In March 27, 1938, the Santa Fe instituted streamliner service to San Diego with the introduction of their new streamliners called the *San Diegan*. In 1939 the Naval Training Center grew by leaps and bounds until it was busting

at the seams. The Marine Corp, sharing the same facility, needed more room for maneuvers so moved north to Rancho Santa Marguerita north of Oceanside, and was renamed Camp Pendleton, after a former commandant of the United States Marines.

Just prior to World War II, San Diego became a military town. Camp Kearney at Linda Vista became the Miramar Naval Air Station. North Island Naval Air Station on Coronado Island replaced the Naval Supply Depot. Military personnel rode Santa Fe's passenger trains and special troop trains between San Diego and Los Angeles.

It was at this time that Bob Hale was transferred from the Panama Canal Zone to the Naval Training Center as a Petty Officer - Fire Control. He found all kinds of trains and locomotives running around the San Diego region and warmed up his camera. Most of the scenes in this book were taken after Bob's

A southbound *San Diegan* crests the Sorrento Grade at Linda Vista station. During World War II, this was a busy place with Miramar Naval Air Base east of the station. Note the order boards have been removed. - N35700

With an ALCO PA unit on the head end, twelve cars of the *San Diegan* wind down the Sorrento Grade from Linda Vista. After a while the round tail end cars were removed. - N35997

The heavy grade between Del Mar and San Diego was known by several names. It was called the Sorrento Grade, the Miramar Grade, Elvira Grade, the Soledad Grade and the Linda Vista Grade. What ever you call it, the grade was tough. In this scene, the *San Diegan* winds around the serpentine track. - N35706

The station platform at the San Diego depot shortly after World War II. To turn the train around required taking the train to National City. So, Santa Fe turned the train at a aircraft plant just north of San Diego. - N35959

The last steam power to seriously challenge the diesel was built during World War II, the Santa Fe's 2900-class. This is one of Bob Hale's classic nighttime scenes at the San Diego depot. - N35958

course at Art Center School of photography. It was his second tour of duty and during the Korean War became Chief Petty Officer - Photography. During his spare time he followed the Santa Fe rails up the coast and practiced his nighttime railroad photography.

At the end of the Korean conflict he resigned from the Navy and tried a hand at commercial photography.

Robert Hale took this spectacular photograph of the Santa Fe's *Chief*, as it snakes through the curves just west of Summit way back in 1952. The eastbound track had a easier grade. The original line is alongside the train and takes off near the end of the *Chief.* - N35711

SANTA FE'S
Run Over Cajon Pass

The Los Angeles bound *Grand Canyon Limited* rolls down the south side of Cajon Pass behind No. 2929. The train has just cleared Blue Cut and is headed for Keenbrook. Note the variety of cars between streamlined to standard which was characteristic of the *Grand Canyon Limited*. - N35810

In the 1880's the Santa Fe was building west toward Southern California under the banner of the Atlantic & Pacific Railroad. At the same time the California Southern Railroad (sponsored by the Santa Fe) based at San Diego, was building north from San Diego to meet the Santa Fe somewhere to the north. In order to build north the road had to pass through Temecula Canyon, and a climb over Cajon Pass in order to reach the desert.

While California Southern forces were grading from the San Bernardino side, crews were grading on the north side, coming together just below Summit on November 9, 1885. They built it as a single track line, the route was soon double-tracked due to increasing traffic.

When the San Pedro, Los Angeles & Salt Lake Railroad was completed on April 26, 1905, the Salt Lake Route obtained trackage rights over the Cajon Pass between Dagget and Riverside.

Due to the heavy grades over Cajon Pass, helpers were used to push freight trains over the pass or to pull passenger trains up the grade from either side, the serpentine tracks and the rock formations of Cajon Pass offered the photographers a challenge.

Bob Hale had photographed the Sorrento Grade, the shoreline around Del Mar, and nighttime shots around the San Diego depot, which had been worked over many times, so he moved north to Cajon Pass. Hale was not married, so spent many a weekend between San Bernardino to Victorville. With the Santa Fe and the Union Pacific operating trains, Hale had a field day.

At Summit he met night relief operator, Chard Walker. Also single, Chard was a telegrapher by vocation and a railroad buff by avocation. Chard was living in the Railroad Booster club house called the *Descanso*, from 1947-1955. The *Descanso* was a former Los Angeles Railway funeral car hauled to Summit just prior to World War II. The car was equipped with all the comforts of home. It contained bunk beds, a table and chairs, cooking stove, ice box, and a coal heater.

The *Descanso* became Hale's weekend home for several years, and a base for his photographing trains all over Cajon Pass. When Bob began to court his future wife, Margaret, his visit began to become few and far between. After their marriage on August 18.1955, they stopped altogether.

Locomotive No. 3776, with 80-inch drivers, wheels the *Scout* westbound through Devore. The town of Devore was named for John Devore, a land developer who hoped his planned community would become a garden spot. - N35862

Two freight trains pass one another on a bridge over Cajon Creek at Devore. Diesel helpers push a tank car train toward Cajon station and Summit. Cajon Creek could become a raging torrent when it rains in the mountains. - N35996

Bob Hale had to climb several hundred feet up a dusty road to obtain this shot of a freight working its way between Keenbrook and Blue Cut, shown in the distance. Cajon Creek squeezes through Blue Cut and begins to spread out as it works toward San Bernardino. - N35919 (LEFT) Locomotive No. 3776 was a regular on the *Scout* or the *Grand Canyon Limited* during the last days of steam at Blue Cut. - N35861

From the same spot on the mountain side, Bob Hale pointed his camera to the south, showing a freight train clearing Keenbrook. In diesel days, freights did not have to stop for water. - N35920

Bob Hale climbed to the summit of Cleghorn Mountain to capture, on film, this scene of Cajon Station below. Cajon Station had an operator at the time and was the split where the eastbound line separated from the southbound route. The eastbound line is identifiable from Cajon to the left, around Sullivan's Curve which is visible. - N35909

Amidst the wild and gloomy rock formations of the San Gabriel Mountains, the *Chief* works its way around Sullivan's Curve, named after a Placentia orange grove rancher who took pictures of steam in the late 1930's. Cajon Pass is not a pass but a division between two mountain ranges. - N35720

First generation diesel locomotives, painted blue amd yellow, works a freight train around Sullivan's Curve in 1955. Southern Pacific Palmdale cutoff destroyed the mystic rock formations when the Southern Pacific built the line from Palmdale to Colton. - N35745

At 3:30 P.M. train No. 22, the *El Capitan*, an all-coach train, works its way up Cajon Pass at Pine Lodge. Note the two water tanks of Cajon Station in the center of the scene at the left. - N35701 (UPPER LEFT) Locomotive No. 3879, a 2-10-2, rolls down Cajon Pass from Summit. Note the brake smoke as brake shoes hit the wheels. - N35881

Santa Fe's *Chief* has just worked around Sullivan's Curve and heads up Cajon Pass, toward Mormon Rocks in 1950, named after the location of a Mormon Colony, years and years ago. The track to the right is the westbound line. - N35922

First generation diesel freight locomotive, No. 202 works a mile long freight train up the southside of Cajon Pass in 1950. - N35733

One of a kind diesel passenger units was No 90, a three unit Fairbanks-Morse locomotive. Shown here with the *Chief* just below Summit in 1950. - N35728

In the early afternoon, the *Chief* approaches the Summit of Cajon Pass. At this point, the eastbound and westbound line come together once again. The westbound line is in the foreground and takes off at the left. - N35712

At 7:03 A.M., the *Grand Canyon Limited* clears Summit, and begins the ascent down the grade of Cajon Pass. This scene was made in June 1950, the sun was already up. - N35707

Santa Fe's *Mail and Express* train No. 7, rolls down Cajon Pass more than four hours late due to rain in the east. The sun is just coming up as No. 3766 rolls down the westbound line at dusk. - N35858

At 4:00 P.M., the *El Capitan* approaches Summit from the west. The *El Capitan*, an all-coach train is carrying three head-end cars. - N35698

Summit of Cajon

The Summit station, circa 1950. The little station of Summit was moved here from Kincaid in the 1940's. All the operators houses are located behind the diesel locomotive on Railroad Avenue, so named by Chard Walker. This scene from the Hale camera shows all the track patterns and crossovers. The eastbound line passes close to the station. The track up the hill to the right was used by helpers pushing the caboose up the hill. The helpers would run down the hill at speed, then the caboose would slowly run down to the end of the train without the helpers. The mountain behind the signal, which is straight up, is Mount Baldy. The tracks at Summit was the only flat place for miles around. The *Descanso*, Bob Hales' Cajon hangout is off to the right, up the hill. - N35739

Diesel helpers crawl along as they pass the Summit station. They will stop a short way ahead, back up the helper cut off track, uncouple the caboose, then run ahead, crossing over, leaving the caboose to couple to the freight. - N35730

Helpers No. 3880 and 3856 roll by Summit station and are about to cut off for a run up the caboose gravity track. The rear brakeman is walking on the engine tender. - N35885

An eastbound freight with no helper on the rear end passes Summit station and the operators houses. The disk on the coupla was some sort of a machine to pass along signals. - N35899

In the 1950's, Chard Walker hands up orders to B. Parkinson, the fireman of extra No. 3858, as it moves eastbound with a freight train. - N35977

The winter of 1952 was a wet one at Summit. Chard had to get out in the cold snow to pass orders to a Union Pacific freight. Sometimes the conductor grabbed the whole hoop containing the orders. - N35975

Receiving message from the dispatcher in San Bernardino, Chard Walker, the nighttime operator at Summit, finds that the message coming through for some other station. Note the Remington typewriter which typed all caps. - N35970

An overall view of Summit, circa 1950. Looking south, the serpentine track rolls through with a first generation diesel on the head end of a long freight. Note one leg of a wye just beyond the fence. The Summit Post Office is the little building beyond the wye. - N35732

The eastbound *El Capitan* rolls through Summit at 4:00 P.M. The silver stand to the left of the *El Capitan* was a sign which read TRAIN which flipped up when the train reached a certain point climbing the grade. There was generally a maintenance-of-way crew which kept the tracks in perfect order. - N35982

The *California Limited*, running three hours late, steams through Summit behind No. 2929. The train was due at Summit at 3:42 A.M. and it is 6:50 A.M. Daylight Savings Time in June. - N35747

After pulling out of Summit, the westbound *Grand Canyon Limited* is about to roll down grade. The fireman looks back to see if his train is still there! - N35844 (BELOW) In a few seconds No. 3759 charges ahead, while passing the throat to the Summit station wye. Note the cattle guards which kept cows off the main line tracks. - N35847

Summit in Snow

Who says it never snows in Southern California. The winter of 1952 was a wet one and it snowed several times on Cajon Pass. It does snow every year a few inches, but not enough for a snow plow. Bob Hale was fortunate enough to be at Summit during a snow. Santa Fe diesel No 264 rolls past the station on its eastbound run. The caboose escape track may be seen behind the telephone pole. - N35937

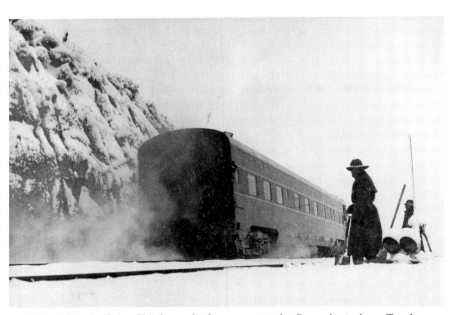

A 4-unit freight diesel on the right prepares to head westbound down Cajon Pass with San Bernardino as its destination. Passenger diesel No. 44 on the *Chief*, is pulling into the Summit yard tracks. - N35937

The tail end of the *Chief* rounds the corner to the Summit station. Track crews were on hand to clear out the switches of ice. - N35936

In 1950, Summit received a dusting of snow during the night. In this scene F7 No 255 rolls westbound through Summit with one of the last stock trains. In earlier times cattle were loaded at the stock pen in the background. - N35749

On the north side of Cajon Pass, No. 3760 with the westbound *Fast Mail & Express* - train No. 7, rolls toward Summit, circa 1950's. Often train No. 7 operated in several sections. During the Christmas season the train would often be in eight to ten sections. - N35854

The East Side of Cajon Pass

Another section of train No. 7 approaches Lugo on the north side of Cajon Pass. The grade was much easier on this north side (or the desert side) compared to the west side. - N35716

No. 2916 rolls down the eastside of Cajon Pass with a way freight. Note the fireman and someone else is in the cab window. The extension stack dejected smoke from above the cab so as not to suffocate the engine crew. - N35773

An oddity of the desert is the gaunt, grotesque Joshua tree, a species of desert foliage in abundance in California's Mojave Desert. They are found on the eastern slope of Cajon Pass all the way to Barstow. Near Hesperia, the short

Grand Canyon Limited heads up the eastside of Cajon Pass behind No. 2916. - N35775

Just outside of Victorville the westbound track crosses over the eastbound line at Frost. In this scene the eastbound *El Capitan* was photographed streaking along at dusk. - N35756

Photographed through a forest of Joshua trees, No. 2922 was photographed by Bob Hale near Lugo, on the eastside of Cajon. - N35781

The eastbound *Fast Mail & Express* whistles for a grade crossing in Hesperia behind an Electro-Motive F7 diesel - N35718

The westbound 14-car *Chief* has just left Victorville and was photographed crossing over the eastbound line at Frost. Victorville is just behind the notch in the hills behind the last car of the train. - N35754

The eastbound *Chief* also at Frost. Note the forest of Joshua trees along the right-of-way. There are homes and a lake in the background in this scene today. - N35943

Train No. 8, the *Fast Mail & Express* works its way eastbound at Frost behind No. 3782. In the 1950's the area was covered with squatter desert shacks among the Joshua trees. Apparently the noise of the passing trains failed to bother the residents. - N35866

Union Pacific's *City of Saint Louis* steamliner departed San Bernardino at 12:20 P.M., and was photographed here just below Summit at 1:15 P.M. behind helper No. 7019, a Mountain type steam locomotive. The steamer was cut off at Summit, then backed down to San Bernardino for another helper run. - N37461

UNION PACIFIC

This scene, near the same location as on the page opposite, shows helper locomotive No. 5093, a 4-10-2 type, moving the *Los Angeles Limited* just below Summit station. Three Fairbanks-Morse diesel units are the regular motive-power on this train. The westbound or descending line takes off to the left near the end of this train. - N37452

The third transcontinental railroad to arrive in Southern California was the San Pedro, Los Angeles & Salt Lake Railroad, which began life as the Los Angeles Terminal Railway. The terminal was a local railroad that ran from Los Angeles to Pasadena, Glendale, Long Beach, Terminal Island, and Pomona. The Salt Lake Route built west from Salt Lake City, and connected with the Los Angeles Terminal west of Riverside.

When San Pedro was absorbed by the city of Los Angeles, San Pedro was removed from the name of the railroad and it became the Los Angeles & Salt Lake Railroad or the Salt Lake Route.

The Salt Lake Route was built by Senator William A. Clark with the financial help of Edward H. Harriman. It was then merged into Harriman's Union Pacific Railroad. The Union Pacific built several branch lines around Southern California, but because its' arrival was late, it never reached the impact of the Santa Fe or Southern Pacific.

The Salt Lake Route had initially planned its own trackage from Yermo to Riverside, by building a long tunnel under Cajon. Due to lack of funds because of ever increasing costs of construction, the Salt Lake Route obtained trackage rights over the Santa Fe from Daggett to Riverside. The tunnel was never built and trackage rights are honored to this day.

Freight and passenger traffic over the Union Pacific never reached the volume as compared with the Santa Fe or the Southern Pacific until the coming of Union Pacific's streamliner fleet in the late thirties with the *City of Los Angeles*, the *City of Saint Louis*, and the *Challenger* economy trains.

The Union Pacific ran some big motive-power on their Los Angeles to Salt Lake main line, such as big articulateds, gas turbines, and huge diesel-electric locomotives.

When Bob Hale tired of the San Diego scene, and moved on to the Cajon Pass scene, apparently the line from Los Angeles to San Bernardino did not interest him. He also never made a nighttime view of a Union Pacific train in Los Angeles Union Passenger Terminal, but he made up for this lack over Cajon Pass to Victorville. He was fortunate to cover the last of steam, and steam helpers on the Union Pacific's Los Angeles to Salt Lake line.

Since its inception, the *Challenger* often operated in three sections during the summer season. The train reached San Bernardino at 9:45 P.M. In this scene, another Bob Hale time exposure, shows a cow-and-calf helper being coupled up to the *Challenger* for the eastbound trip up Cajon Pass to Summit. This time exposure shows the helper crew alongside their charge. - N37325

The Challenger

The *Challenger* was an all-coach economy train established in 1935, with coffee shops-lounge car and economy diner. Following World War II, the train was streamlined with dome cars. In the mid-1950's the *Challenger* was only operated from June 1 to September 5, and during the peak midwinter holidays.

On the tail end of the *Challenger* at San Bernardino station, the conductor with lantern in hand, about to swing the "All Aboard." - N37521

42

Helper engine No. 5023, a powerful 4-10-2 type, assists an eastbound freight up Cajon Pass, just beyond Cajon station, as it nears Sullivan's curve. The three ALCO FA's are working hard as well as No. 5023 whose boiler is ejecting steam. - N37443

Rails over Cajon

Union Pacific's prime Los Angeles to Chicago train, the *City of Los Angeles*, works its way around Sullivan's Curve, at dusk, without a helper locomotive on the head end. - N37302

Four American Locomotive Company FA (freight units) drag a mile long freight train around the scenic Sullivan's Curve. Note the black soot stains on the four diesel units which was due to the ALCO engines which smoked a great deal, almost like a steam locomotive. - N37314

Electro-Motive 1400-class diesel units work the Farmer John pig stock train from Summit to San Bernardino down the westside of Cajon Pass. The train is just about to reach Cajon station, out of sight at the left. Special Farmer John's pig trains brought fresh hogs to the Farmer John Packing House at Vernon, two days per week. Fresh hogs were picked up in Iowa and transported to Los Angeles. This special stock movement was the last of the stock trains. The eastbound track up Cajon Pass takes off at about the third stock car. - N37312

Union Pacific helper engine No. 7019 coasts its way down to San Bernardino after helping a train up the hill. Union Pacific helpers chose to back down to San Bernardino, where as Santa Fe helpers turned on the Summit wye and were returned to San Bernardino the right way. - N37463

Snow turned the rather drab countryside at Summit into a fairyland. In this scene, freight train No. 1634 was working a freight train westbound past the Summit station for preparation of the descent of the westside of Cajon to San Bernardino. - N37317

Two Union Pacific helpers, Nos. 5093 and 5095, have just shoved up a freight up the westside of Cajon Pass. The two engines will soon cross over to the down track and back down to San Bernardino. - N37459

A Union Pacific switcher (the cow-n-calf) bring the *City of Saint Louis* up the westside of Cajon and slowly works past the Summit station, while a crew member on the ground cuts off the helpers. The three Fairbanks-Morse road units will take the train east. -N37323

A Fairbanks-Morse *Trainmaster* unit helps the *Los Angeles Limited* eastbound up Cajon Pass as it approaches Summit station. The track on the left is the westbound or down line of Cajon. - N37309

47

The sun was hardly up this morning, when an eastbound Union Pacific special pulled up to the Summit station for orders. Apparently this special was a rail enthusiasts special. Note all the people standing alongside the station. - N37301

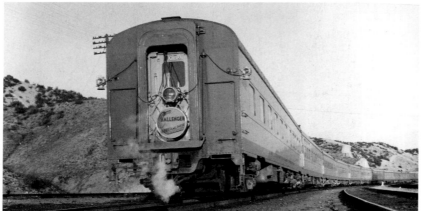

The eastbound *Challenger* pulls up to the Summit station, a little early, for orders. It is 2:35 P.M. and the rear brakeman is protecting the rear end of his train out of sight. - N37468

Here is lots of activity at Summit station. The *City of Saint Louis* pulls out, while the Union Pacific helpers are on the escape track with two Santa Fe helpers. Note the helper (steam) to the left of the streamliner, and another in the distance. - N37477

Freight extra No. 1627 clears Summit and prepares to descend the westside of Cajon Pass. Note all the black stains on top of the ALCO units due to the excess smoking. Note the Santa Fe wye which takes off to the right. - N37319

At 10:45 P.M., Chard Walker, the night operator at Summit station, hands up the order hoop to the fireman of Union Pacific train No. 38. This is the ALCO experimental units returning eastbound that were shown in the Los Angeles Union Terminal section. - N35687

Robert Hale took this unique photograph from an overhead walkway at Green River, Wyoming. The passenger train is apparently the *Challenger*.

UNION PACIFIC MAIN LINE
Ogden to Cheyenne

Union Pacific gas-turbine No. 56 waits for an eastbound run at the Ogden round-house, in 1955. The gas-turbines on the Union Pacific were known as the "Big Blow" because of the noise they produced. A separate fuel tender was provided on long runs. The turbines were an experiment that provided more horsepower per foot of locomotive, but required constant maintenance. Crew said that beyond the noise the locomotives produced, they rode like a Pullman. - N37240

There are few railroads that evoke the legend of early American railroading as does the Union Pacific, the eastern half of the transcontinental railroad. Today, the Union Pacific has become the largest railroad in the United States.

On Bob Hale's trip around the United States in search for the last of the steam locomotive, he moved from Cajon Pass to Utah and Wyoming. Together with his wife Margaret, Bob covered the Wyoming Division running from Ogden to Cheyenne, the mountain country of the Union Pacific. Here were heavy grades and wide open spaces of the Great American West. It was on this race track of trains that Bob photographed giant 4-6-6-4-type engines and the huge 4-8-8-4-type locomotives, better known as the "Big Boy," the largest steam locomotives in the world. There are also interesting experimental gas-turbines and fast moving 4-8-4-type locomotives once used exclusively in passenger service.

Union Pacific's double-track main line from Omaha to Ogden was a race track. You did not have to wait for more than ten minutes and Bob would find a train rolling either east or west.

Even without the steam locomotive, the Omaha to Ogden main line is still one fast super railroad.

Just east of Ogden, Utah, was a heavy grade known as Weber Canyon. The grade raised the Union Pacific 2,445 feet, from 4,298 feet at Ogden to 6,745 feet at Evanston, Wyoming, the summit of the grade. In this scene, gas-turbine No. 57 leads a freight train up Weber Grade. Dual steam helpers were pushing the freight from the rear. - N37241

Part of the way up the grade was Devil's Slide station, at 5,251 feet. This view finds gas-turbine No. 69 on the head end of a stock train stopped for some reason. Why the front door is open remains a mystery, possibly to collect cool air. - N37250

Helper No. 3704 pushes a freight near the top of the grade at Washatch. - N37337 (TOP LEFT) A 4-6-6-4 type, No. 3786 was photographed pushing a freight up the grade as it passes the Castle Rock sign. Helpers were cut off at Evanston, Wyoming, and returned back down the grade to Ogden. - N37355

Working its gut out pushing a freight up the grade, No. 3701, another 4-6-6-4 type, pushes a freight up Weber Canyon. - N37329

This three-quarter view of No. 4013, the World's Largest Steam Locomotive, shows the vast size of the locomotive at Green River, Wyoming. - N37410

At Green River, Wyoming, "Big Boy" No. 4015, a 4-8-8-4 type, has just taken on a full tender of coal and heads for the ready track. Bob Hale took this photograph from an overhead walkway across the yard tracks. - N37413

Bob Hale caught No. 4009 articulating through yard switches at Green River. No. 4009 has just dropped its charge in the yard behind, and is heading for the coal chute for another run. - N37396

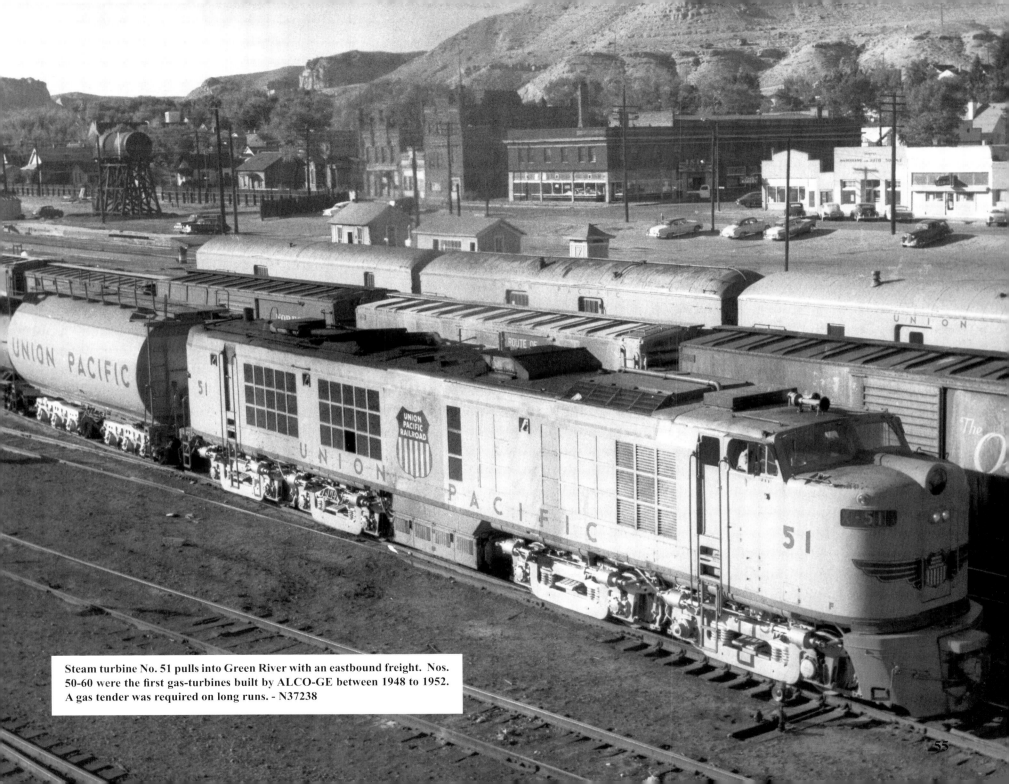

Steam turbine No. 51 pulls into Green River with an eastbound freight. Nos. 50-60 were the first gas-turbines built by ALCO-GE between 1948 to 1952. A gas tender was required on long runs. - N37238

Bob Hale spent a couple of days at Green River. In this scene finds streamliner the *City of Los Angeles*, changing crews at the Green River station. While making this photograph a gas-turbine pulls in under the yard walkway, while en route to the yard in the distance. - N37505

Down at the large coal chute, find "Big Boy" No. 4016 moving for a load of coal for the tender. - N37252

Just below the overhead walkway, Bob Hale found gas-turbines Nos. 58 and 52 wheezing away. - N37506

It is 135 miles between Green River to the Rawlins engine terminal. "Big Boy" locomotives Nos. 4019 and 4020 are at the coal chute. - N37518 (LEFT) A giant 4-6-6-4 type 3969 has taken on a load of coal in its tender and ready for a run. - N37374 (RIGHT) No. 4000 moves down the right-of-way to hook on to its train. - N37378

Bob Hale's specialty was the panned railroad shot. He would hang out the window of the car, panning along with the train, then shooting it at a slow shutter exposure. In this view, Nos. 809 and 839 roll the *Fast Mail & Express* between Rawlins and Medicine Bow. - N37680 (LEFT) Engineer Ted Jenkins in the cab of a 3900-class locomotive. - N35727 (BELOW) A reefer train of California produce charges the main line between Rawlins to Medicine Bow. - N37511

Union Pacific passenger train headed by No. 842, climbs the eastside of Sherman Hill at dusk, producng this spectacular photograph. The shot was taken from a signal ganty.

After leaving Borie, just ten miles west of Cheyenne, finds "Big Boy" No. 4011 charging a westbound stock train at the foothills of Sherman Hill. In the days before super highways, the Lincoln Highway followed the Union Pacific main line out of Cheyenne, for a short distance. - N37403

Rolling down the westside of Sherman Hill find No. 4017 rolling its way down to Laramie from Summit. This train is a solid fruit block. The distance between Cheyenne and Laramie is 54 rail miles. - N37422

Working its way west, a gas-turbine No. 62 pulls out of Cheyenne yard and passes Cheyenne Tower on the westside of the town of Cheyenne. Note the huge airplane parts on the flat car just behind the locomotive. - N37248

Locomotive No. 3703, a 4-6-6-4 type, waits at Cheyenne for a run up the eastside of Sherman Hill. - N37334 (LEFT) A portrait of a "Big Boy," with No. 4017 at the Cheyenne roundhouse and shops.

"Big Boy" No. 4013 leaves Cheyenne Tower in the dust, as it begins to climb up the eastside of Sherman Hill with a freight. - N37409

(RIGHT) At a highway overpass, Bob Hale photographed train No. 57 the Denver connection. The train will travel to Borie, where the Denver main line cuts in. - N37294

At Los Angeles Union Passenger Terminal, postal workers rush to load mail bags aboard Railway postal cars of the Los Angeles to San Francisco all-Pullman *Lark*, train No. 75, which left the station at 8:00 P.M.

The *Coast Daylight*, running between San Francisco to Los Angeles, arrives at dusk at Los Angeles Union Passenger Terminal. Locomotive No. 4458 moves slowly from Mission Tower to the Inner Tower. - N36907

SOUTHERN PACIFIC

There is no easy route into and out of California in order to tap the great wealth west of the Rocky Mountains. No matter from what direction the Southern Pacific built, it had to find its way over and through the mountains of the Coast Range.

The Southern Pacific was the first major main line railroad to operate in California. From the start the Southern Pacific dominated the railroad scene, both passenger and freight, and the Southern Pacific controlled many business properties such as milling, lumbering, mining, rock and gravel products.

Within California, the Southern Pacific had the most routes of railroad operation. It had the Coast Line, the San Joaquin Line, the Sunset Line, the Golden State Line, the Shasta Line, and the Overland Line which was its portion of the Central Pacific Railroad.

For 123 years, the Southern Pacific brought more individuality to the design and operation of their locomotives. The Southern Pacific operated more passenger and freight trains than anyone else, had a vast ferry service across San Francisco Bay, and for years was California's largest employer.

Southern Pacific traffic within California had the steepest grades to cover such as the Cuesta Grade of 2.2 percent on the Coast Line. The most severe operating conditions were encountered by SP's San Joaquin Valley Line over Tehachapi Pass, and the route east over Donner Pass with its snowsheds and over 100 inches of snow fall per year.

The following pages are presented as a photographic sampling of Robert Hale's journey as he saw it.

Just two miles north of Mission Tower, along the shore of the Los Angeles River, was Taylor Yard, the principal yard of Los Angeles. Established in 1908, it was expanded in 1913, and became a major yard of Southern California by 1923. It contained a huge freight roundhouse, major shops, and a Pacific Fruit Express repair facility. In this unique photograph, Bob Hale walked across the massive bridge across the many yard tracks to capture this scene of the hump yard.

There were two terminals for motive-power on the Southern Pacific. One was the Los Angeles General Shops where passenger power was maintained, and Taylor Roundhouse and shops where freight power was kept. With the decline of steam, a huge diesel shop was built on the west end of Taylor yard. This scene, taken at night, shows the variety of diesel power.

After arriving from Electro-Motive, No. 5671, a GP-9 is being inspected by a Taylor Shop worker. This locomotive is in pristine condition, and was painted in red, orange, black and silver print scheme.

Bob Hale had access to the Taylor diesel shops and found No. 6381, an F-7, going through the locomotive washer. Several years down the road the locomotives became so dirty one could hardly read the road name. The emblem was a metal plate screwed onto the locomotive.

When Bob Hale finally got around to photographing Santa Susanna Pass, around the Chatsworth area, steam had been displaced on the *Coast Daylight*. In this scene, ALCO PA's in the 200 series (original numbers) were working the westbound (to San Francisco) *Daylight* as it passes through the Chatsworth rocks area of Santa Susanna Pass. The ALCO PA's were eventually renumbered into the 6000 series. - N36615

A brace of road diesels carry a eastbound piggyback train through the Chatsworth rocks of Santa Susanna Pass. After leaving the region the train will roll through the San Fernando Valley in order to reach Los Angeles. - N36959

The Los Angeles bound *Lark*, an all-Pullman sleeper train, rolls through the Chatsworth rocks about 8:15 A.M. with arrival at Los Angeles at 9:25 A.M. - N37103

No. 622 an F-7 hood unit, with an extra odd-ball mixture of six baggage cars and several box cars rolls by Corrigan Ranch on the west side of Santa Susanna Pass. The long Chatsworth tunnel is off in the distance. - N36974

A refrigerator block of California lettuce moves toward Los Angeles as it rolls through Chatsworth Rocks of Santa Susanna Pass. - N37105

COAST LINE

Among the most scenic lines of the far-flung Southern Pacific empire is the Coast Line running between Los Angeles and San Francisco. The Coast Line was built in bits and pieces, and was finally completed in 1901.

The Coast Line is rich in agricultural produce from plums, to oranges and lemons, sugar beets, strawberries and grains. The rich Santa Clara Valley contains miles and miles of fruit trees. Salinas has its garlic, and the Simi Valley and San Fernando Valley rich in fruits and grains. A third of the route makes a mad dash along the shores of the blue Pacific, just feet from the foaming surf.

Southern Pacific Coast Line carried its famous train, the *Coast Daylight*. Classified as the "Most Beautiful Train in the West," with its red, orange and black livery, as vivid as California's setting sun. Two complete trains were built to provide daily service. It became so popular that a *Noon Daylight* was inaugurated.

The all-Pullman sleeping car train, the *Lark*, running between Los Angeles and San Francisco-Oakland complimented the *Daylight's* schedule.

Extra No. 5656 east wraps itself around horseshoe curve between Goldtree and Chorro, as part of Cuesta Grade, with a solid train of sugar beets. At this time they were starting to put extra sides on the beet cars. - N36957

SAN LUIS OBISPO

The town of San Luis Obispo, a small railroad town in the beginning, was based at the foot of the Santa Lucia Mountains. Its excuse was a helper station to raise the twisted rails over Cuesta Grade. Based here was a large roundhouse full of helper locomotives during the steam era. San Luis Obispo is at 240 feet and Cuesta Grade raised the rails to 1,295 feet at Cuesta.

In the diesel era San Luis Obispo is not as busy as it once was, however diesel locomotives still help freights up Cuesta and help brake freights down the west side today.

Five GP-9's brake a long freight down Cuesta Grade near Goldtree. This mile long train, stretching in the distance, has three helpers on the rear end to help brake the train so that it does not runaway down the grade. - N36955

During mid-morning, a westbound freight travels west on the corkscrew grade at Goldtree. Three helpers were attached to the rear of the freight at San Luis Obispo to help boost this freight up Cuesta Grade. The helpers will be cut off at the top of the grade at Santa Margarita. Some helpers are running back to San Luis Obispo for future service, some remained at Santa Margarita to help a freight down Cuesta Grade. - N36998

San Jose to San Francisco commuter train No. 137 left San Jose at 6:00 A.M. with arrival time at San Francisco at 7:35 A.M. with 19 stops en route. Speedster No. 4300 was handling the train this day when Bob Hale took this photograph in the early 1950's. - N36795

SAN FRANCISCO - SAN JOSE PENINSULA
COMMUTER SERVICE

Following World War I, citizens began to spread down along the Peninsula to have a bigger home with a yard, finally reaching San Mateo and San Jose. Businessmen required passenger service to their offices in the city, and shoppers needed service to San Francisco stores. Commuter service taxed the double-track main line between San Francisco to San Jose, with commuter runs mixed in with main line passenger and freight operations. The line saw commute runs to San Francisco in the morning hours, and commute runs to San Jose in the afternoon and early evening.

Commuters were carried in sparten coaches, which were mainly a shell with uncomfortable seats, called Harriman cars. After years of complaints that commuters were handled like cattle, the Southern Pacific purchased several double-deck cars in the late 1940's to handle the 8,000 commuters. The Southern Pacific stated that hauling commuters was a money losing proposition. The State of California took over the operation in 1980 known as Caltrain.

A midday commuter train leaves San Jose bound for San Francisco. Most midday trains carried women en route to San Francisco for a day of shopping. - N37093

An engineer leans out of the cab window of No. 4370, a 4-8-2 type. He waits for the "All Aboard" signal from the conductor at San Francisco's 3rd & Townsend Station. - N36841

With diesel power on the head-end of a group of Gallery cars, backs in to the 3rd & Townsend Station for a commute run to San Jose. - N36952 (LEFT) An overall view of San Francisco's 3rd & Townsend Station in the afternoon. Note all the commute trains lined up in the station without locomotives. - N36822

At 5:00 P.M. in the afternoon, four locomotives are lined up for their runs to San Jose. This was the last hurrah for Daylight 4-8-4's, and 4-8-2's. This photograph was taken in the early 1950's. - N37077

Train No. 168 rounds the curve outside of 3rd & Townsend Station at 3:05 P.M. bound for San Jose behind locomotive No. 4355, a hefty 4-8-2 type. - N36831

The 4:20 P.M. commute run to San Jose pulls out "on time" behind semi-streamlined No. 4307, a 4-8-2 type. Galley cars carried a third more commuters than the Harriman cars. - N36801

Southbound commute train No. 112 leaves the 3rd & Townsend Station in the early afternoon with three Harriman commute cars in tow. - N3667

With 80-inch drivers digging into the rails, as No. 4457, still in *Daylight* paint scheme of orange, red and black, pulls out of the San Jose station with the westbound *Lark*. This train is due in San Francisco at 9:30 A.M. - N36904

The eastbound *Coast Daylight*, train No. 98, left San Francisco at 7:45 A.M. and is now pulling into San Jose at 8:50 A.M. The locomotive on the right is backing down into the San Jose station for a run to San Francisco. - N36908

The westbound *Lark* pulls out of San Jose station bound for San Francisco at 8:20 A.M. as the observation car rolls by. - N37046

At dusk, a piggyback train pulls out of San Francisco for the overnight run to Los Angeles. All trailers, at this time, belong to subsidiary Pacific Motor Trucking, circa early 1950's. - N36958

This is the time exposure that won Bob Hale a Graflex photographic award. The straight line in the background is California State Highway Route No. 58 which runs from Mojave to Bakersfield. All the other lights are a Southern Pacific eastbound train which began at the left, which is Woodford, and then climbs the grade, goes around the loop, then passes in the foreground while en route to Tehachapi summit and Mojave. - N35679

This is a photograph of an eastbound Santa Fe freight with a four-unit diesel that produced 6,000 horsepower. It approaches a bridge just below the loop, will pass under the loop itself, will encircle the loop and proceed on to the town of Tehachapi. California State Highway No. 58 is the line behind the train. - N36004

TECHACHAPI PASS
Southern Pacific - Santa Fe

One of the seven wonders of the railroad world is California's famous Te-hachapi Pass and the "Loop." Here the rails of the Southern Pacific (now Union Pacific) and Santa Fe (now Burlington Northern Santa Fe) breast Tehachapi Pass between Bakersfield and Mojave.

The railroad route over Tehachapi Pass was built between 1875 and 1876. The celebrated "Loop" made possible the lifting of the grade 2,734 feet from the base range to the summit of the pass itself 20 air miles away and 3,969 above sea level.

The construction of the Tehachapi Pass line involved miles of track laid through abysmal gorges and along narrow shelves in mountain country and through many tunnels, climaxing at the "Loop" where long trains pass over themselves as they circle a cone shaped hill. In 8.7 miles uphill from the "Loop" the rails of Tehachapi Pass reach the town of Tehachapi and the summit. The rails then drop 1,243 feet in 18.3 miles before reaching Mojave and desert country.

When the Santa Fe purchased Southern Pacific's Mojave to Needles Line, they obtained trackage rights from Mojave to Bakersfield.

Southern Pacific diesel unit No. 6386 and three other units take train No. 52, the eastbound *San Joaquin Daylight* around the loop. This train is only moving at 20 miles-per-hour. - N36991 (BELOW) This is an excellent view of the loop itself. It shows eastbound train No. 52, the *San Joaquin Daylight* looping around the loop with double-headed steam power. A 4300 type is on the point as a helper and the road power is a Daylight 4-8-4 type. - N37121

These two photographs were taken atop the cone of the Tehachapi Loop looking down on a Santa Fe freight and its helper working its way to the loop itself. (UPPER LEFT) Santa Fe No. 3843, a 2-10-2 type, is working a fruit block eastward. - N35875

After helping a Southern Pacific freight up the Tehachapi grade, cab-forward No. 4203 returns to Bakersfield for another helper run. The locomotive has rounded the loop and is about to pass under the loop track itself. - N36745

The westbound *San Joaquin Daylight* has just encircled the loop and prepares to dip under the loop itself. It is double-track around the loop and then goes back to single track. - N37118

An eastbound Southern Pacific freight crosses over the bridge below the loop itself, will pass under the loop tracks, then will encircle the loop itself. Note the freight above this train already going around the loop. - N37130

An eastbound Santa Fe freight passes under California State Route No. 58 at Woodford. At this point there are two long passing tracks besides the single track main line. - N35740

After encircling the loop, Santa Fe locomotive No. 266 makes its way toward Tehachapi and Mojave. The Loop Ranch, located in the middle of the loop itself, may be seen behind the locomotive. - N35751

At midtrain finds Santa Fe GP-7's shoving No. 266 up the Tehachapi grade. The rear portion of this freight appears to be a fruit block. - N35763

A major earthquake struck the Tehachapi area on July 12, 1952 causing tracks to be thrown out of alignment and the caving in of several tunnels. A massive reconstruction was taken on a 24-hour basis of daylighting several tunnels and realigning the right-of-way. In this scene, an eastbound Santa Fe freight was photographed moving eastward by August 15, 1952. - N36015

On the *San Joaquin Daylight*, helper locomotive No. 4352 assists the road power, a 4-8-4. It is moving eastward at Woodford. - N36825

The caboose end of a westbound Santa Fe freight passes the Woodford water tank. - N35900

At the same location, road units have just passed through tunnel No. 12 near Marcel, while en route to Tehachapi and Mojave. - N35738

(OPPOSITE PAGE) The brakeman of train No. 373, a time freight, leans out the gangway of locomotive No. 3672, a 2-10-2 type, rolling eastbound up the San Joaquin Valley.

Rolling eastward, Santa Fe road unit No. 200 curls around the serpentine grade. The train has just passed through tunnel No. 12 en route to Tehachapi. - N35731

The new and the old at Fresno yard. The 0-6-0 switchers were working around the clock, and smaller power was used on the various branch lines bringing in cars for sorting in the Fresno yard. A 1950's built F-7 diesel freight unit waits for a main line run. - N36988

Fresno, the world's "raisin center" and principal marketing and shipping point of the San Joaquin Valley, contains a large yard, roundhouse and engine maintenance facility. In the view above, a 3700-class starts out with a long eastbound freight from Fresno. - N37145 (RIGHT) Fresno yard contained a variety of power during the steam era. There were many branch lines operating out of Fresno. - N36730

San Joaquin Valley

Train No. 51, the streamlined *San Joaquin Daylight*, speeds up the San Joaquin Valley from Fresno to Modesto. The locomotive, No. 4421, was once decorated in orange, red and black paint, with skirts and other trappings, and is now all locomotive black. In the late 1940's and early 1950's when locomotives went in for general repair, they were stripped of their beauty. - N36859

The *Sacramento Daylight*, a beautiful streamliner running between Los Angeles and Sacramento was installed in 1946. Cars were attached to the *San Joaquin Daylight* at Los Angeles, and cut off and ran as the *Sacramento Daylight* at Lathrop. The *Sacramento Daylight* operated as trains Nos. 53 and 54. In the above scene, two cars from train No. 54 are attached to the rear of the *San Joaquin Daylight*. - N36670 (RIGHT) The *San Joaquin Daylight*, train No. 51 still in Daylight colors, pulls up to the cutoff point at Lathrop. Engine No. 2475 will then take the *Sacramento Daylight* on to the capitol city. - N37021

Southern Pacific No. 3275 whisks a local freight between Lathrop and Tracy along the flat San Joaquin Valley. This is another of Bob Hale's panned shots. - N36713

Two giant cab-forward freight locomotives are headed eastbound as they pull into Tracy. No. 4211 is a time freight train No. 551. Tracy has been a junction point since the town was laid out in the early 1870's. It is the junction of the mid-valley line to Fresno and the east line to Lathrop and Sacramento. Tracy was also a pick-up point for freight from the surrounding region. - N36747

After leaving Martinez, No. 4163, a 4-8-8-2 type cab-forward locomotive takes a long fruit block up the grade from Martinez to Suisun Point, then crosses the double-track Martinez-Benicia bridge. In this scene, the train shirts through a Standard Oil tank farm. - N36732

The *Shasta Daylight*, an all-coach daily streamliner running between the Oakland Mole and Portland, Oregon, crosses the Martinez-Benicia bridge. The Carquinez Straits are shown in the background. The *Shasta Daylight* is en route to Davis, where the train will head north to Portland. - N37033

The Sacramento to Oakland local train No. 247, the *El Dorado*, has just crossed the Martinez-Benicia bridge while en route to Martinez and the Oakland Mole. - N36668

Carquinez Straits is eight miles long and a mile wide at it narrowest point. It carries the waters from the Sacramento and San Joaquin rivers into San Francisco Bay. A double-track main line runs from the Oakland Mole, Richmond, Sacramento, all the way above Auburn. In the view above, locomotive No. 2816, a C-9 2-8-0 type, rushes a short freight along the Straits bound for Richmond. - N36704 (RIGHT) Another train on the double-track line along the Straits is No. 4412 as it moves a mile long freight near Crockett. - N36854

Three GP-9's and another locomotive, painted in their orange, red, silver and black livery, are hooked up to a long train of Pacific Motor Trucking trailers are hooked to scheduled freight No. 374 at Richmond during the mid-1950's. - N36953

A long string of Pacific Motor Trucking piggyback trailers take off from Richmond, bound for some unknown location. - N37090

Piggyback train No. 374, taken on another day, prepares to run eastbound from Richmond with a long string of Pacific Motor Trucking trailers. In the early 1950's most piggyback trailer trains were PMT trailers. - N36954

Freight No. 2475 rolls toward Richmond from Crockett with a short freight. This photograph was taken from a moving automobile following along as a semi-panned shot. - N36675

At 8:14 A.M., the southbound *San Joaquin Daylight* pulls into Richmond to pick up passengers for valley points and Los Angeles. The fireman has left his cab and is standing in the gangway. - N37030
(RIGHT) Train No. 51, the northbound *San Joaquin Daylight* rolls into Richmond at 6:18 P.M., bound for Oakland Pier. - N36893

All trains in transcontinental service on both the Southern Pacific and Western Pacific began and ended at Oakland Pier or Mole. The long barn like structure was dark and dingy. In this scene, the *San Joaquin Daylight*, train No. 51, prepares for its run to Los Angeles. Baggage and mail handlers hustle to load their cars before train time. - N36862

After a short rain in the early evening, Bob Hale spotted this reflection in the Oakland Yard and made a time exposure. Locomotive No 4360 is reflected in the standing water.

After pulling out of Oakland Pier, train No. 51, the *San Joaquin Daylight* pulls out of the cavernous shed and passes Oakland Pier Tower. - N36873

Oakland - San Francisco

In order to reach San Francisco from the Oakland Pier, passengers were required to take a Southern Pacific ferry trip across San Francisco Bay. Ferry boats ran in conjunction with transcontinental trains. - N37003

Ferry boat trips across San Francisco Bay were run in conjunction with train schedules. It took 30 minutes for a ferry to cross the bay. In this scene, the steamer *Berkeley* is pulling into the mole at San Francisco's famous Ferry Building. - N37076

Sausalito, on San Francisco Bay, was the southern terminus of the Northwestern Pacific Railroad, a wholly owned subsidiary of the Southern Pacific. Sausalito once was a busy place with commuter trains running in and out, and passenger ferries crossing the bay. There were also freight car barges carrying freight to Sausalito bound for northern points. In this 1950 scene, finds Southern Pacific diesel No. 1902 looking for business. - N36643 (LEFT CORNER) A barge loaded with freight cars makes its way toward Sausalito. - N35906

NORTHWESTERN PACIFIC RAILROAD

The Northwestern Pacific Railroad came into being in 1907 as a consolidation of some 40 narrow-gauge and standard gauge railroads. The NWP was the creation of the Santa Fe and Southern Pacific railroads to handle redwood lumber from Eureka to San Francisco Bay points. The Northwestern Pacific Railroad also ran a commuter train service from Marin County to San Francisco.

The Northwestern Pacific was part narrow-gauge from Sausalito to Cazadero, its standard gauge lines from Sausalito through the coast counties of Marin, Sonoma, Mendocino and Humbolt to Eureka, in the heart of the Redwood Empire.

Before the Golden Gate Bridge was built, the Northwestern Pacific operated electric commuter service into Sausalito, and carried passengers across the bay in ferry boats. Once the bridge was completed commuter traffic began to fall off, and the service was eventually abandoned.

Also due to the Eel and Russian rivers running rampant at various times, and the tearing out the right-of-way, the Northwestern Pacific lost its redwood lumber business.

In the early 1950's, the Pacific Coast Chapter of the Railway & Locomotive Historical Society ran an excursion over the Northwestern Pacific Railroad starting at Sausalito and running north to an unknown location. Bob Hale, while working in northern California learned of the trip and decided to photograph the train. In the above scene, No. 183, a 4-6-0 type works a train with railfans sticking out from any open door. - N36505 (LEFT) Watch the drivers roll! Green jacketed, sporting a link-and-pin coupler, Southern Pacific 4-6-0 No. 2248 was loaned to the Northwestern Pacific for a last run fan trip. No. 2248 makes an engaging sight as she gallops along on the Northwestern Pacific. - N36507 (BELOW) Locomotive No. 183 somewhere out on the line. - N36503

Donner Pass

The Southern Pacific tamed the great American deserts and crossed more mountain ranges than any railroad in the United States. "King of the mountain grades" was Donner Pass. Everything about Donner Pass was monumental: the grade, the locomotives, the tonnage handled and snowfall at Norden which could reach 100 inches per year.

The Donner Pass Line was Central Pacific's end of the Transcontinental Railroad, connecting Sacramento with Ogden, Utah and meeting of the Union Pacific at Promontory in 1869.

Bob Hale, while working in Northern California for several years, never took more than two photographs of the Donner Pass Line. Why no one knows. He missed a lot of scenic areas, but two are shown here.

In the scene at the left, diesel units, with No 6232 on the point, on a westbound freight working upgrade on the old line, exits tunnel No. 6 just east of Norden at the summit, between wooden snow sheds. Down in the valley below, is Donner Lake. - N36987 (ABOVE) Just east of Roseville finds cab-forward racing eastward up the Donner Pass Line with a 100-car freight. - N36757

Southbound freight No 554, with locomotive No 4252 on the head end pulls up to the water spout at Alturas. After filling the tender with water, the train will take off for the Likely Loop and eventually Wendell. - N36764

A standard 2-8-8-4 AC-9 steam locomotive rests in the Sparks roundhouse ready for service on the Modoc Line. Nos. 2800-2811 were brought from the New Mexico Division where they were coal burning locomotives to run out their years on the Modoc Line. The No. 3805 had been converted to burn oil. - N36723

MODOC LINE

The Modoc Line, was a short cut route built between the main route east-west line at Fernley, Nevada, and ran a line to Klamath Falls, Oregon, and a connection with the Cascade Line. It was surveyed in 1911 and was built from Fernley to Susanville in 1912 to haul out the forest products. It was extended north to Klamath Falls in 1926 over part of a narrow-gauge railroad known as the Nevada-California-Oregon Railway.

The Modoc Line, named after Modoc County, Oregon, was a short cut route from Portland to the east in order to run in competition with the Western Pacific-Great Northern "Inside Gateway." Between Fernley to Alturas was mostly semi-desert country. South of Alturas, and north of Sage Hen, was a huge loop which carried the rails of the Southern Pacific several feet known as the Likely Loop. The Modoc Line was for freight service only, and never carried any passenger trains.

Just 59 miles south of Alturas, finds No. 4252 at Ravendale Station to pick up orders. The fireman is climbing back into the cab. - N36742

Cab-forward No. 4211 on train No. 551, and two helpers on a 100-car freight train, works its way around the Likely Loop. The trains moved very slowly while rounding the loop tracks. - N37017

(LEFT) The train above works its way around the loop. -N37010 (ABOVE) The third engine and the caboose works its way around the loop. - N36999

A northbound freight with No. 6259 on the point, moves through Odell Lake while moving downgrade to Eugene and Portland. The tracks more or less follows the middle fork of the Willamette River in this tall timber country. - N36983

A northbound freight, with an odd mixture of motive-power, rolls into Cascade Summit while en route to Oakridge and Portland. - N36979

Helpers were used for braking while rolling down the canyon, as well as to help lift trains up the grade. In the view above, helper No 4253 provides braking power on the freight train as it rumbles through Wicopee station. - N36773 (RIGHT) Cab-forward No. 4253 helps brake this freight as it rustles down the Cascades. N36771

Extra No. 3718 works downgrade through McCredie Springs which is along Salt Creek. - N36721 (LEFT) As this freight works its way down the Cascades, helper No. 4263 provides additional braking power. - N36780

CASCADE LINE

The new Cascade Line was opened on August 7, 1926, which provided the Southern Pacific a short low-grade line between Black Butte, California, on the Shasta Route and Eugene, Oregon. The old Siskiyou Line was crooked as a dogs hind leg and required considerable time to navigate.

Through the barrier of the mighty Cascade Mountain Range, the Southern Pacific created a new route via Klamath Falls, Crescent Lake to Eugene.

Diesel cab unit No. 6259, breaks the silence of the canyon as it clatters across Salt Creek viaduct on its journey to Eugene. (LEFT) Helper No. 4263 comes down at mid-train providing additional braking power. - N36781

A 1,750 hp. GP-9 road unit on the head end of time freight No. 636 is working hard as it climbs the grade on the Cascade Line out of Eugene at night.

At Oakridge, helper No. 4197 waits under steam for a southbound or eastbound run up the hill. - N36742

With steam escaping, cab-forward No 4259 patiently waits for a run at Eugene. - N36778 (LEFT) Three-unit diesel-electric units with No. 6338 on the point, heads in to Abernethy station while en route to Klamath Falls. - N36981

While photographing the Southern Pacific Pipeline under construction on the Golden State-Sunset Route, Bob Hale took a moment to photograph passing trains. In this scene on Beaumont Hill, he found the second section of the Golden State Route passenger, train No 43, climbing westbound near Cabazon, with three-cylinder No. 5036 on the point. - N36939

Extra freight No. 6244, an F-3 Electro-Motive F-3 diesel units, climb Beaumont grade near White-water (Cabazon) with a two-mile freight train. - N36977 (RIGHT) On the rear of the above diesel freight is No. 4354 helping push the freight up Beaumont Hill. - N36829

Beaumont Hill

Sitting in the hoghead's seat of an eastbound freight, finds Bob Hale taking a picture of a westbound freight with U25B's on the headend.

Southern Pacific No. 3930, a former Verde Tunnel & Smelter 2-6-6-2 from Arizona, was acquired by the Southern Pacific in 1943 for helper service on Beaumont Hill. In this scene, No. 3930 and a 5000-class three-cylinder locomotive, work their way toward Indio for a run back up the hill. - N36725

Another view of the Golden State Route passenger train No. 43, working its way west on Beaumont Hill. On the point is No. 3625, a 2-10-2 built by Baldwin in 1919. - N.36914

Narrow-gauge No. 9 races north from Keller to Oweyno in this panned photograph. At this point on the line the highway runs close to the track. Mount Whitney, the highest point in the continental United States is just behind the steam dome. - N36596

Taking on a load of water at Keeler at the southern end of the line, No. 9 has a load of ten cars of talc and an extra water car in its consist. The fancy headlight and fake cabbage stack were installed for a movie and had not been removed. - N365921

Southern Pacific Narrow - Gauge

(FAR LEFT) The standard gauge Line Pine Branch ran from the main line at Mojave to Oweyno, a distance of 143 miles. In this scene, narrow-gauge and standard gauge meet. No. 5505 is an RSD-5 which worked the daily train. - N36603 (BELOW) On the run from Keeler to Oweyno, the narrow-gauge train is dwarfed by the mighty Sierra Range. - N37213

Primary products shipped on the narrow-gauge during its twilight years were abrasives and talc. Carborundum was loaded into narrow-gauge gondola cars and unloaded into standard gauge gondola cars at Oweyno. - N37190

Steam locomotive No. 9 is kept warm all night by the hostler at Oweyno for the next days run. The fake headlight and the cabbage stack were installed for a movie.

Talc, used for women's face powder, was loaded into sacks at Keeler, and hand transferred to standard gauge box cars at Oweyno. - N37186

Old coaches were used for cabooses on the Southern Pacific narrow-gauge. The car on the right lost its monitor roof in a fire and was replaced with a flat roof. - N37196

En route from Keller to Oweyno, No. 9 looks like a speck in the distance at Mount Whitney station. The wye here was used for storage of cars. - N37219

No. 9, working its way north to Laws, passes Manzanar station siding. Manzanar, you will remember, was the location of the Japanese Enternment Camp during World War II. - N38184

Narrow-gauge engineer Ferguson at the throttle of No. 9. Strange as it may seem, he worked out of the Salt Lake Division, while the branch was part of the San Joaquin Division timetable. - N37224

A photograph of No. 9, taken from the top of the water tank at Laws yard. Note the outhouse in the upper right hand corner of this photograph. - N36605

Southern Pacific diesel No. 1 was photographed switching the Sierra Talc plant at Keeler. No. 1 was built new for the Southern Pacific in 1954. It was also the only narrow-gauge diesel ever built for a common carrier in the United States. - N37182

Northbound extra No. 1 pulls up to the Mount Whitney siding, just south of Oweyno with three cars of talc for transfer at Oweyno. - N36585

No. 1, bound from Keeler to Oweyno, approaches the Mount Whitney siding. - N36587

Railroad Photography

This book was designed and written by Donald Duke
for Malcolm McCarter. The text and captions were
prepared by Ruth Rodgers, who also scanned the photographs
used in this book. The photographs are from the collection of
Malcolm McCarter. The printing was done by offset lithography
by Walsworth Publishing Company of Marceline, Missouri.